A World of IMAGINATION

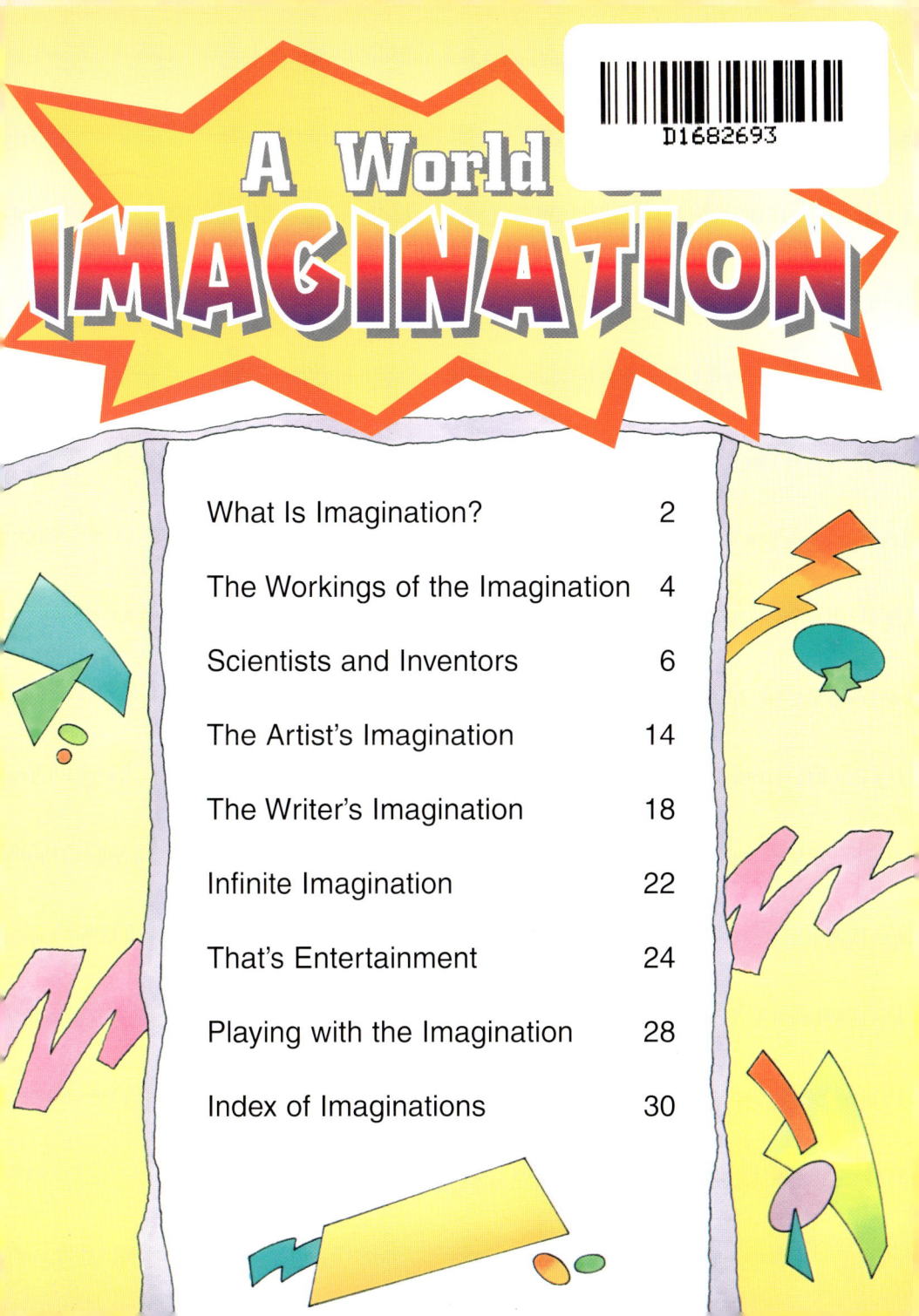

What Is Imagination?	2
The Workings of the Imagination	4
Scientists and Inventors	6
The Artist's Imagination	14
The Writer's Imagination	18
Infinite Imagination	22
That's Entertainment	24
Playing with the Imagination	28
Index of Imaginations	30

What Is Imagination?

Everyone has an imagination. It's a world we visit in our minds while our bodies stay put. Sometimes it might seem we are doing nothing when, in fact, our minds are busily creating an endless variety of scenarios. In the world of imagination, we can be whoever we want and go wherever we please.

Visits to the world of imagination are a crucial part of our existence. Without imagination, life would be very different.

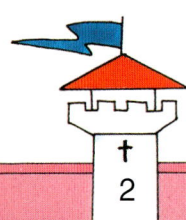

A LEAP OF THE IMAGINATION

Engrossing books, thrilling films, new inventions, stunning buildings, and beautiful works of art are all the results of people putting their imaginations to creative use. Even when we invent something like a new combination of ingredients for a sandwich, or try out a different hairstyle, we are being imaginative. It's hard to imagine the world without imagination!

The Workings of the Imagination

Where is the imagination located, and how does it work? Most people would agree that the imagination is in the brain. We don't have to be a track and field pro to imagine what it might be like to be a famous athlete. Our brain remembers pictures we have seen of great athletes, and at the same time, recalls what it felt like when we did something well. It combines these thoughts and memories to enable us to imagine we are the world's best athlete.

An Active Imagination

The pictures we create in the mind are vivid, even though they might not exist in reality. When we read a book or listen to a story, our imagination is hard at work creating mental images. The images television presents, however, replace the personal pictures we create in our minds. Being constantly given "the picture" makes fewer demands on our imaginations. So it is important that we keep our imaginations stimulated by reading books, creating things, and exploring problems.

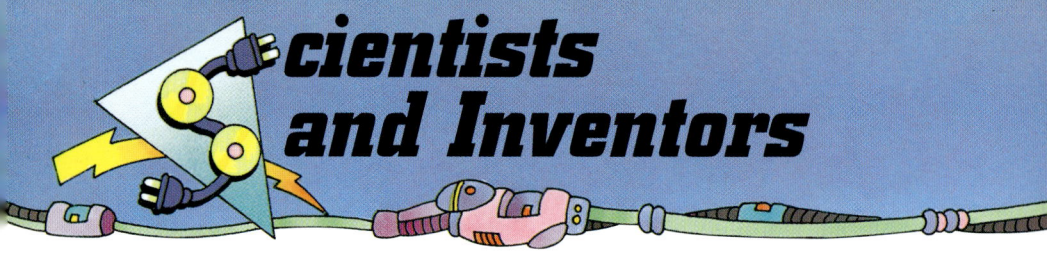

Scientists and Inventors

Inventors use imagination, observation, curiosity, knowledge, and determination to make their dreams come true.

Sir Isaac Newton (1642–1727)

At eleven years old, Isaac Newton was behind in school. He went on to become a great scientist, famous for inventing the theory of gravity. The idea came to him as he saw an apple fall in his mother's orchard.

Newton also studied light and color, and found that white light is made up of all the colors in the rainbow.

Albert Einstein *(1879–1955)*

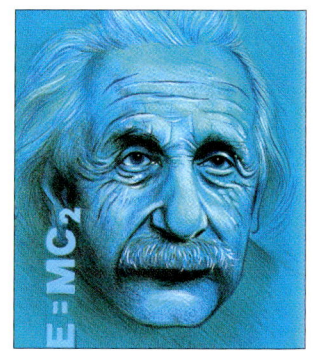

Many people believe Albert Einstein was the most creative thinker ever. Yet he was unable to speak clearly until he was nine years old. When he was five, he became intrigued by a pocket compass. He wanted to know why the needle always pointed north. Einstein went on to develop extremely complicated theories. His theory of relativity states that when you travel very fast, time slows down. Einstein is thought to have said: "Imagination is more important than knowledge."

Marie Curie (1867–1934)

Curie was an imaginative and studious child. Her view that "we must believe that we are gifted for something, and that this thing, at whatever cost, must be attained" helped her to develop her gifts for physics, chemistry, and mathematics.

Using her imaginative intelligence, Curie was able to visualize the existence of two unknown elements. It took nearly four years of hard physical and mental work before she proved she was right. She named her discoveries *polonium* and *radium*, and invented the word *radioactivity* to describe their behavior.

Curie was the first woman to win a Nobel Prize. In fact, she won *two* – one for physics and one for chemistry.

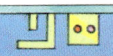

Alexander Graham Bell (1847–1922)

As a child, Alexander Graham Bell dreamed of becoming a famous pianist, but, instead, he chose to help deaf people to speak. His studies of voice led him to a fascination with sound, then an interest in electricity.

In 1874, Bell sat at a spot he called "the dreaming place" on the Grand River in Bradford, Ontario, and let all his thoughts and ideas about electricity and sound run through his head. Suddenly, everything came together, and he knew how he could make a telephone. Despite the fact that the scientific information had been available for fifty years, no one had come up with the idea of a telephone before.

Bell was the first person with both the knowledge of these scientific fields and the imagination needed to create a practical application.

Thomas Edison (1847–1931)

When Thomas Edison started school, he asked so many questions that his teacher thought he was stupid. Although his teacher didn't realize it, Edison's questions were a sign of a curious and imaginative mind. Later, Edison went on to register 1,093 inventions, including the first practical electric lightbulb and a record player.

As an adult, Edison's aim was to think up one minor invention every ten days and one "big trick" every six months. When someone tried to cheer Edison up when he was having trouble inventing the storage battery, Edison replied, "I haven't failed. I've just found ten thousand ways that it won't work."

The Artist's Imagination

The most famous artists have been people who used their imaginations to find original ways of expressing their thoughts and emotions. They developed their own styles instead of following the fashions of their time.

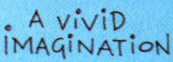  

Pablo Picasso (1881–1973)

Picasso's artistic talent was noticed when he was nine years old. Many of Picasso's paintings show people and scenes that look distorted and out of perspective. They are in an artistic style called *cubism*, in which the artist shows many different angles of a scene or subject in a single work of art. It is up to the people looking at the art to identify the different shapes and put the scene or subject back together in their minds.

15

Maurits Escher (1898–1972)

Escher was an artist who liked to use his imagination to puzzle and amaze people. He was fascinated with the idea of infinity. Many of his pictures show patterns that seem to repeat themselves forever.

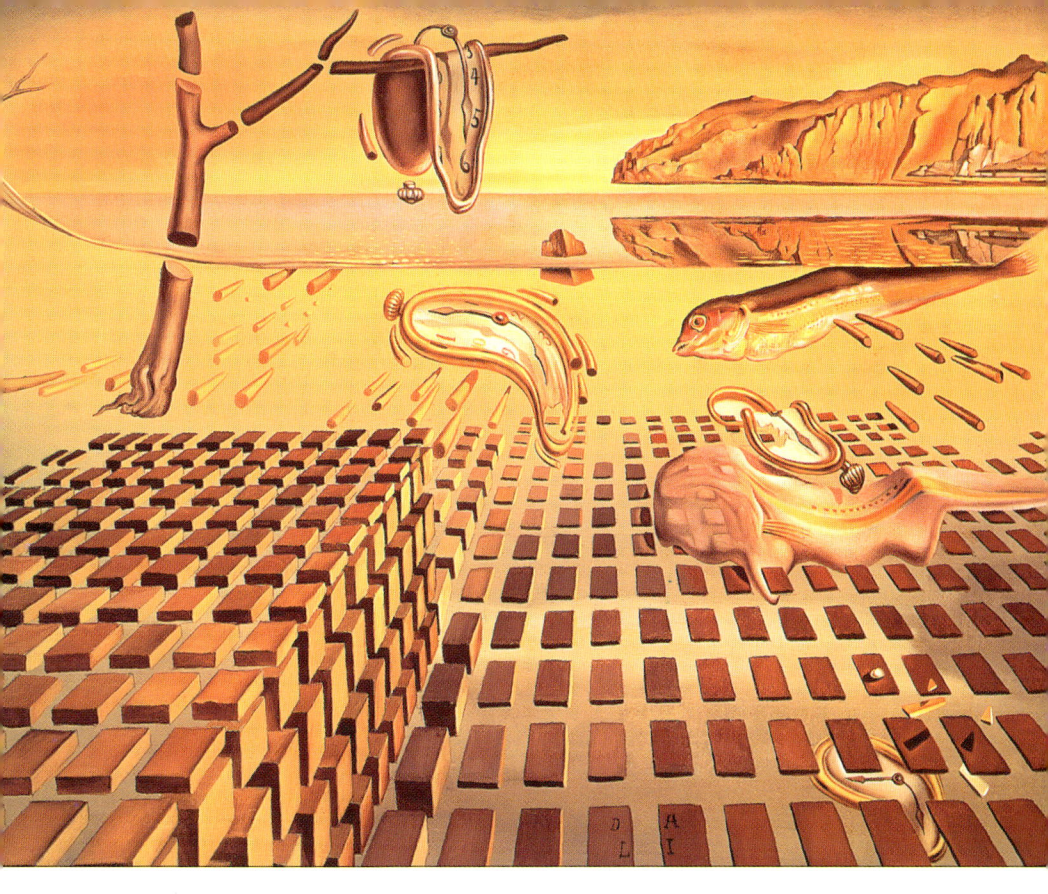

Salvador Dalí (1904–1989)

Dalí called his pictures "handpainted dream photographs." Many of his works remind people of nightmares. They often include insects and disjointed parts of human bodies.

The Writer's Imagination

Some of the most well-loved books are those that take the reader into imaginary worlds.

C. S. Lewis (1898–1963)

In C. S. Lewis' *Narnia* series, four children are able to enter the magical land of Narnia by walking through the back of a wardrobe.

Jules Verne (1828–1905)

In his science-fiction books, Jules Verne dreamed up adventures and inventions, such as a rocket trip to the moon, one hundred years before the events took place. Verne was not a scientist, but he tried to make his books very realistic. The underwater boat in *Twenty Thousand Leagues Under the Sea* is very similar to the modern submarine.

19

J. R. R. Tolkien (1892–1973)

J. R. R. Tolkien's book *The Hobbit*, the first in a series of books describing a world named Middle-earth, is full of weird and frightening creatures.

"The Mad Hatter's Tea Party," illustration (by Arthur Rackham) to *Alice's Adventures in Wonderland* by Lewis Carroll (1832–1898), British Library, London/The Bridgeman Art Library, London.

Lewis Carroll (1832–1898)

Alice, of the famous story *Alice in Wonderland*, was a real person. But everything else in this tale comes from the imagination of Lewis Carroll. Alice follows a rabbit down a rabbit hole into a place full of strange creatures and bizarre situations. Some of the poems in the book don't make sense, but they are fun to read.

Carroll

Infinite Imagination

Many authors start from a base of facts and research and then apply their imagination to write a story.

Rachel Carson (1907–1964)

Rachel Carson, a twentieth-century author, could convey her feelings about her scientific observations through her imagination. Her book *Silent Spring* tells of an imaginary town where the plants and animals start to die, people become sick, and a silent spring occurs because there are no birds left. Many of her predictions have come true in parts of the world.

Gerald Durrell (1925–1995)

When Gerald Durrell was a child, he became fascinated with wildlife. *My Family and Other Animals* is the story of the fun he had comparing friends and family with the animals he observed. By applying an imaginative writing style to his knowledge of zoology, Durrell has passed on to others his love for nature.

Gerald Durrell (left) and actor Darren Redmayne, who played the young Durrell in a television series about one of his books.

What's Entertainment

Inventors, artists, and writers are not the only people who need good imaginations. Many industries rely on new ideas generated by the people who work in them. The future of a company may rest on an eye-catching window display, an effective advertising campaign, or an imaginative packaging design.

Walt Disney (1901–1966)

Walt Disney began drawing cartoon characters as a child. One of his most famous creations was Mickey Mouse, based on a mouse that shared his office. In Disney's imagination, Mickey became a real person – so real that Disney would tell people an idea couldn't be used, because Mickey wouldn't like it!

Disney ran out of time to draw the cartoons, so he hired a staff of artists and technicians he called "imagineers."

© Disney Enterprises, Inc.

The entertainment business, including movies and television, relies on transporting people into a world of make-believe.

Some of the largest monuments to one person's imagination are Disneyland and Walt Disney World, with its Epcot – all the brainchildren of one man, Walt Disney. Today, Walt Disney's vast amusement parks transport visitors beyond reality on thrilling rides through imaginary "lands." Technological advances, such as holograms, have kept pace with the Disney designers, helping them to create almost anything they can dream up.

Playing with the Imagination

Movies, cartoons, and amusement parks are entertaining products of other people's imaginations. In contrast, toys and games take players into imaginary worlds they create for themselves. The more imagination the players use, the more exciting the game.

Play is an important way in which people develop their imaginations.

wings
of
the
imagination

Some children have used their imaginations to do things other than play games. Becky Schroeder was ten years old when she designed a clipboard that would glow in the dark. The idea for Glo-boards came to her after she wished she could do her homework while waiting for her mother in the car at night.

Our imaginations are a part of us, and they can never be used up. In fact, the more we use them, the better they become. So don't hold back. Let your imagination take flight!

Index of Imaginations

Bell, Alexander Graham   10–11
Carroll, Lewis   21
Carson, Rachel   22
Curie, Marie   8–9
Dalí, Salvador   17
Disney, Walt   24–27
Durrell, Gerald   23
Edison, Thomas   12–13
Einstein, Albert   7
Escher, Maurits   16
Lewis, C. S.   18
Newton, Sir Isaac   6
Picasso, Pablo   14–15
Schroeder, Becky   29
Tolkien, J. R. R.   20
Verne, Jules   19

From the Authors

Judith Hodge   Mary Atkinson

When we sat down to write a book about the imagination, we soon realized how difficult a subject it was. Because the imagination exists inside people's mind, it's very difficult to describe – and impossible to photograph.

We also realized how much imagination is a part of our lives. It was hard to find a topic that didn't involve the imagination in some way.

Finding imaginative people to write about was easy. The problem was deciding which of them to include. We hope reading this book will stimulate *your* imagination.

Imagine That!

Fuzz and the Glass Eye
Which Way, Jack?
The Wish Fish
Famous Animals

Pie, Pie, Beautiful Pie
My Word! How Absurd
You Can Canoe!
A World of Imagination

Written by **Mary Atkinson** and **Judith Hodge**
Illustrated and Designed by **Kelvin Hawley**
Photography by **David Lowe** (pp. 28–29); **New Zealand Picture Library:** (runners, pp. 4–5); **Culver Pictures Inc.:** (Marie Curie, p. 9); **Superstock/VI$COPY Ltd.:** (Picasso painting, p. 15); **Cordon Art:** (Escher painting, p. 16); **Bridgeman Art Library:** Salvador Dalí Museum, Florida (Dalí painting, p. 17); British Library (The Mad Hatter's Tea Party illustration by Arthur Rackham, p. 21); **HarperCollins Publishers:** (The Lion, the Witch and the Wardrobe, Pauline Baynes, p. 18; The Map of Tolkien's Middle Earth, John Howe, p. 20); **Photobank Image Library:** (Disneyland, pp. 26–27); © **Disney Enterprises, Inc.:** (Splash Mountain at Walt Disney World, p. 26; Cinderella Castle at Walt Disney World, p. 27)

Previously published in *Literacy 2000*.

© 1999 Shortland Publications Inc.
All rights reserved. No part of this publication may be reproduced or transmitted in any form or by any means, electronic or mechanical, including photocopying, recording, taping, or any information storage and retrieval system, without permission in writing from the publisher.

05 04 03 02 01 00 99
10 9 8 7 6 5 4 3 2 1

Published in the United States by

a division of Reed Elsevier Inc.
500 Coventry Lane
Crystal Lake, IL 60014

Printed in Hong Kong
ISBN: 0-7901-1832-7